Weather

Kristin Baird Rattini

NATIONAL
GEOGRAPHIC

Washington, D.C.

To Tom and Emily, the sunshine of my life —K. B. R.

The publisher and author gratefully acknowledge the expert review of this book
by Jeff Weber of the University Corporation for Atmospheric Research.

Paperback ISBN: 978-1-4263-1348-6
Library Edition ISBN: 978-1-4263-1349-3

Book design by YAY! Design

Photo credits
Cover, Ron Gravelle/National Geographic Your Shot; 1, Robert Postma/First Light/Corbis; 2, rtem/
Shutterstock; 4–5, Michael DeYoung/Corbis; 6, Flickr RF/Getty Images; 7, Dennis Hallinan/Jupiter
Images; 8–9, Jasper White/Getty Images; 10, National Geographic RF/Getty Images; 11, Sami
Sarkis/Getty Images; 12–13, SuperStock; 14, Radius Images/Getty Images; 15, amana images RF/
Getty Images; 16, Michael Durham/Minden Pictures; 18–19, Na Gen Imaging/Getty Images; 20,
SuperStock; 22–23, LOOK/Getty Images; 24 (UPLE), sittitap/Shutterstock; 24 (UPRT), HABRDA/
Shutterstock; 24 (LO), Mark Lewis/Getty Images; 25 (UP), Minerva Studio/Shutterstock; 25 (LOLE),
Galyna Andrushko/Shutterstock; 25 (LORT), Dainis Derics/Shutterstock; 26–27, Roy Morsch/
Corbis; 28, Varina Patel/iStockphoto; 29 (UP), Miro Photography/First Light/Corbis; 29 (LO),
Richard Bloom/Getty Images; 30 (LE), Ljupco Smokovski/Shutterstock; 30 (RT), Jeffrey Conley/
Getty Images; 31 (UPLE), tale/Shutterstock; 31 (UPRT), SuperStock; 31 (LOLE), irin-k/Shutterstock;
31 (LORT), Juan He/Shutterstock; 32 (UPLE), Dainis Derics/Shutterstock; 32 (UPRT), Michael Durham/
Minden Pictures; 32 (LOLE), Popovici Ioan/Shutterstock; 32 (LORT), Digital Vision/Getty Images

Printed in the United States of America
13/WOR/1

Table of Contents

Look Up at the Sky

The weather helps us know
what to wear, and do, and grow.

It brings rain, wind, and sun.
Let's go outside for some fun!

What Is Weather?

Peek out your window at
the sky. Is it sunny or cloudy?
Rainy or windy? You are
checking the weather!

Weather is what it's like outside at one place, at one time. But keep a lookout. Weather can change fast!

The Sun

The sun warms the land. It warms the air and water, too.

The sun's heat and light help things grow. Plants and animals need sunshine to live.

Sunny days are fun. You can play outside! Will you go to the park? Or ride a bike? The sun can make the air outside hot. You can cool off with a swim!

Clouds

White, fluffy clouds are called cumulus (KYOOM-yuh-lus) clouds.

Tiny water droplets float in the air. They group together. They make clouds of all shapes and sizes.

White, fluffy clouds mean good weather.

Weather Word

DROPLET: A very small bit of liquid

13

Flat, gray clouds
bring rain.

Flat, gray clouds are called stratus (STRA-tuhs) clouds.

Some clouds are
thin and wispy.
They can look
like curls of hair.
These clouds float
high in the sky.

Thin, wispy clouds
are called cirrus
(SIR-us) clouds.

What Comes From Clouds?

Drip, drop. Down comes the rain!

Water droplets in clouds sometimes fall as rain. Rain falls in warm and cool weather.

Rain helps plants and animals live. It fills rivers and ponds. Rain forms puddles on sidewalks. *Splash!*

Weather Word

FLURRY: A light snowfall that barely covers the ground

Brrr! It's cold outside. Water droplets in clouds sometimes freeze. They can fall as hail or snow.

If it's hail, you'll see ice. If it's snow, you might get a flurry (FLUR-ee). Often, a lot of snow means a snow day!

Lightning and Thunder

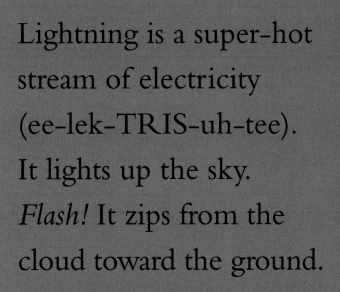

Lightning is a super-hot stream of electricity (ee-lek-TRIS-uh-tee). It lights up the sky. *Flash!* It zips from the cloud toward the ground.

After lightning comes a *BOOM!* That sound is thunder.

Rainbows

Have you ever seen a rainbow after a storm? Rainbows are made from sunlight and water droplets.

Rainbows paint bright stripes of color in the sky. Red, orange, yellow, green, blue, and purple. Which color do you like best?

6 Ways Weather Is Wild

1

Sometimes water flows where it is usually dry. This is called a flood.

2

Hail is ice that rains from the sky. It can be small. Or it can be bigger than a baseball!

3

A hurricane brings heavy rain and strong winds.

4

Very strong winds sometimes twist.
They form a tornado.

Weather Word

BLIZZARD: A heavy
snowstorm with wind

5

It's hard to see in a
blizzard!

6

Sometimes it doesn't rain
for a long time. This is
called a drought
(drowt).

Wind

Wind is moving air. A light
wind is called a breeze. A strong
wind is called a gale.

Wind has energy. It pushes
clouds and rain across the sky.
Wind can make kites dance.

Weather and Me

The weather helps you plan your day. Should you wear sunglasses or rain boots? Will you swim or throw snowballs?

Wherever you go, the weather is always with you.

What in the World?

These pictures are close-up views of weather things. Use the hints to figure out what's in each picture. Answers are on page 31.

HINT: Wear these in sunny weather.

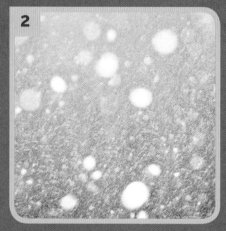

HINT: They fall as a flurry or as a blizzard.

WORD BANK

raindrops snowflakes sunglasses umbrella clouds lightning

HINT: This goes up when rain comes down.

HINT: A stream of electricity

HINT: They come in all shapes and sizes.

HINT: They fall from the clouds in warm weather.

Answers: 1. sunglasses, 2. snowflakes, 3. umbrella, 4. lightning, 5. clouds, 6. raindrops

BLIZZARD: A heavy snowstorm with wind

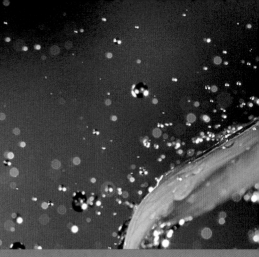

DROPLET: A very small bit of liquid

ELECTRICITY: Energy that can make heat and light

FLURRY: A light snowfall that barely covers the ground